Hal Leonard Student Piano Library

Piano Practice Games

Book 2

Preparation activities for pieces in **Piano Lessons**

- Listen
- Read
- Create

Authors
Barbara Kreader, Fred Kern, Phillip Keveren

Consultants
Mona Rejino, Tony Caramia, Bruce Berr, Richard Rejino

Editor
Anne Wester

Illustrator
Fred Bell

CONTENTS

* Students can check activities as they complete them.

For technical support, email **support@halleonard.com**.

To access audio, visit:
www.halleonard.com/mylibrary

Enter Code
4530-2674-6320-4331

ISBN 978-0-7935-6261-9

HAL•LEONARD®

Visit Hal Leonard Online at
www.halleonard.com

World headquarters, contact:
Hal Leonard
7777 West Bluemound Road
Milwaukee, WI 53213
Email: info@halleonard.com

In Europe, contact:
Hal Leonard Europe Limited
1 Red Place
London, W1K 6PL
Email: info@halleonardeurope.com

In Australia, contact:
Hal Leonard Australia Pty. Ltd.
4 Lentara Court
Cheltenham, Victoria, 3192 Australia
Email: info@halleonard.com.au

Foreword

Piano Practice Games present imaginative ways to introduce pieces in **Piano Lessons** by coordinating technique, concepts, and creativity with the actual music in the lesson book. These preparation activities help focus learning by "playing with" each lesson piece aurally, visually, and physically.

Before each lesson piece is assigned:

Listen & Respond activities develop rhythmic and technical coordination.

active listening

Read & Discover activities reinforce understanding and recognition of musical patterns and symbols.

guided reading

After each lesson piece is mastered:

Imagine & Create activities expand knowledge of newly-learned concepts.

improvising and composing

Whether used in private or group lessons, **Piano Games** are all designed to make music. Many activities include accompaniments that can be added in the following ways:

Teacher

 4

Audio

May you enjoy many happy hours of musical discovery and success.

Best wishes,

Carmen's Tune

(Lesson Book 2, pg. 7)

As you listen to *Carmen's Tune*, tap the following rhythm:

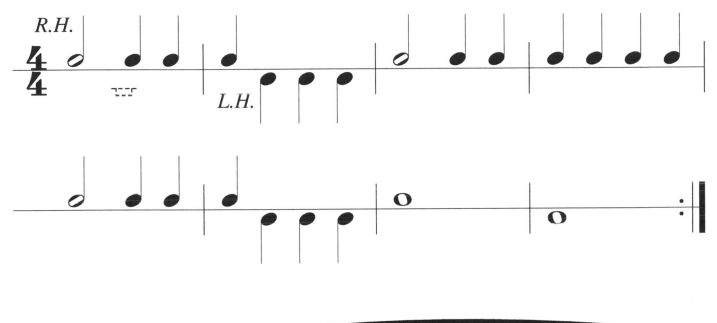

Read & Discover

The Beat Goes On!

When the melody passes from one hand to the other, the beat goes on.
While one hand plays, the other hand rests. Using your lesson book as
a guide, add the missing rests to the rhythm of the melody above.

Andantino

(Lesson Book 2, pg. 8)

Phrases

When a curved line or slur connects several notes, it identifies a PHRASE -- a musical sentence.

Open your lesson book to the score of *Andantino*. As you listen to the music, trace each phrase with your finger. Lift your wrist at the end of each phrase.

Read & Discover

Below are the first four phrases from *Andantino*.

1. Using your lesson book as a guide, add a slur either over ⌒ or under ⌣ each phrase.

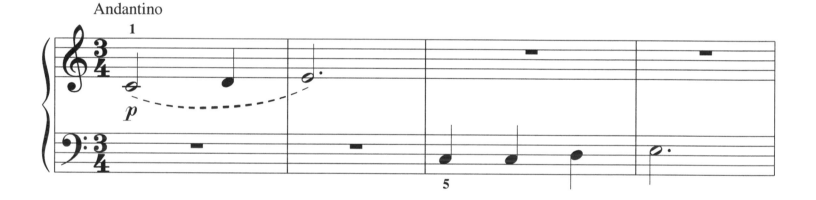

2. As you listen to *Andantino*, sing the melody on "la." Make sure to sing each phrase in one breath.

3. Now play the phrases. Imitate the smooth and connected sound of your singing by playing each phrase LEGATO, passing the sound smoothly from one finger to the next.

4

Echo Phrases

Sometimes a phrase copies the one before it. Using your lesson book as a guide:

1. Write the missing notes in the bass clef.

2. Write the missing dynamics, *forte* and *piano*.

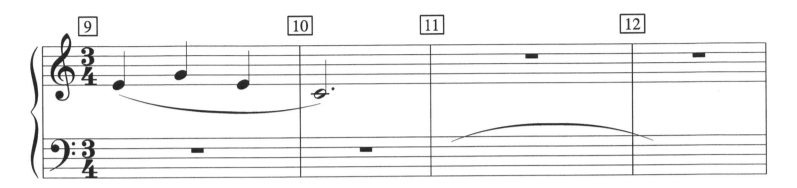

Imagine & Create

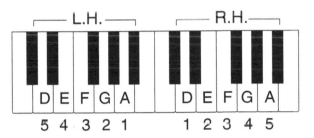

Change the mood of *Andantino!*

1. Place your hands in this position two octaves above middle C. Note that this is one key higher than the *Andantino* position.

2. As your teacher plays the accompaniment below, play *Andantino* in this new position. Use the same finger numbers and keep the shape and rhythm of the melody the same.

Teacher Accompaniment

Listen & Respond

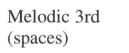

Please, No Bees!

(Lesson Book 2, pg. 10)

**Technique Tunes
by Katherine Glaser**

As you listen to *Please, No Bees!*,
play this **Technique Tune**.

Note: As a duet, the teacher plays "Please, No Bees!" 8va higher.

Read & Discover

Study the score of *Please, No Bees!* in your lesson book. Count how many times each example appears and write the answers in the boxes.

Harmonic Intervals

Harmonic 2nds [   ]   Harmonic 3rds [   ]

Melodic Intervals

Melodic 3rd [   ]
(spaces)

Melodic 3rd [   ]
(lines)

Melodic 2nds [   ]

6

Clapping Song

(Lesson Book 2, pg. 11)

You can create a variation of *Clapping Song* by playing the melody in the bass clef.

1. In the magnifying glasses, write the note names.

2. Using the arrows as a guide, complete the L.H. melody in the bass clef using quarter notes.

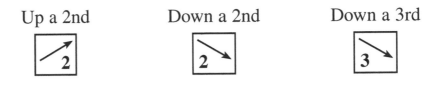

Same   Up a 2nd   Down a 2nd   Down a 3rd

3. Write the name of each note in the blank below it.

4. As you listen to *Clapping Song*, play the melody in this L.H. variation.

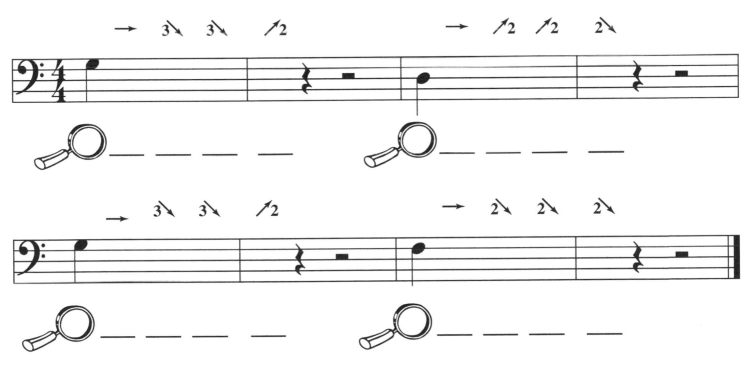

Note: As a duet, the teacher plays "Clapping Song" 8va higher.

Hoedown

(Lesson Book 2, pg. 12)

 5

Technique Tunes
by Katherine Glaser

Join the *Hoedown* as the fiddler by finding the 4ths in each hand. As you listen to the accompaniment, play the following **Technique Tune** one octave higher than written.

Imagine & Create

Can you name this *Mystery Tune*?

1. In the magnifying glasses, write the note names.

2. Using the arrows as a guide, complete the melody using quarter notes.

| Repeat | Up a 2nd | Down a 2nd | Down a 4th |

3. Write the name of each note in the blank below it.

4. Play the *Mystery Tune* and write the title in the blank below.

Title:_____

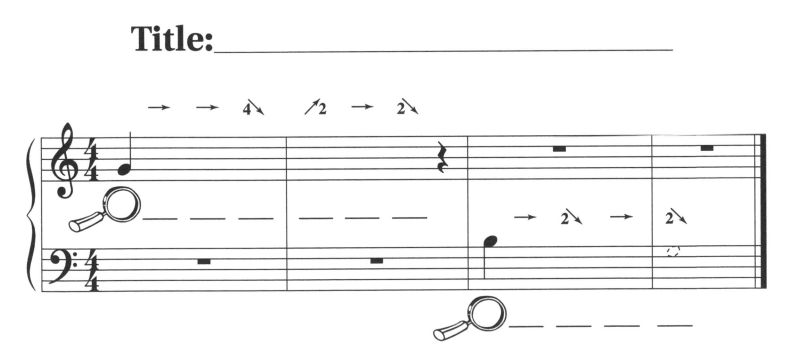

Sunlight Through The Trees

(Lesson Book 2, pg. 13)

Imagine & Create

🔊 6

1. **Put the pieces back together!**

   Cut out the cards on the next page and arrange them in the correct order of the piece, *Sunlight Through The Trees*.

2. **Create a new piece!**

   Begin with the card showing the clef signs and the time signature.

   Arrange the groups of notes in any order you wish.

   Place the card with the double bar at the end of the piece.

3. **Give your composition a title!**

   Save your new piece by taping it on a piece of cardboard.

Title:_____

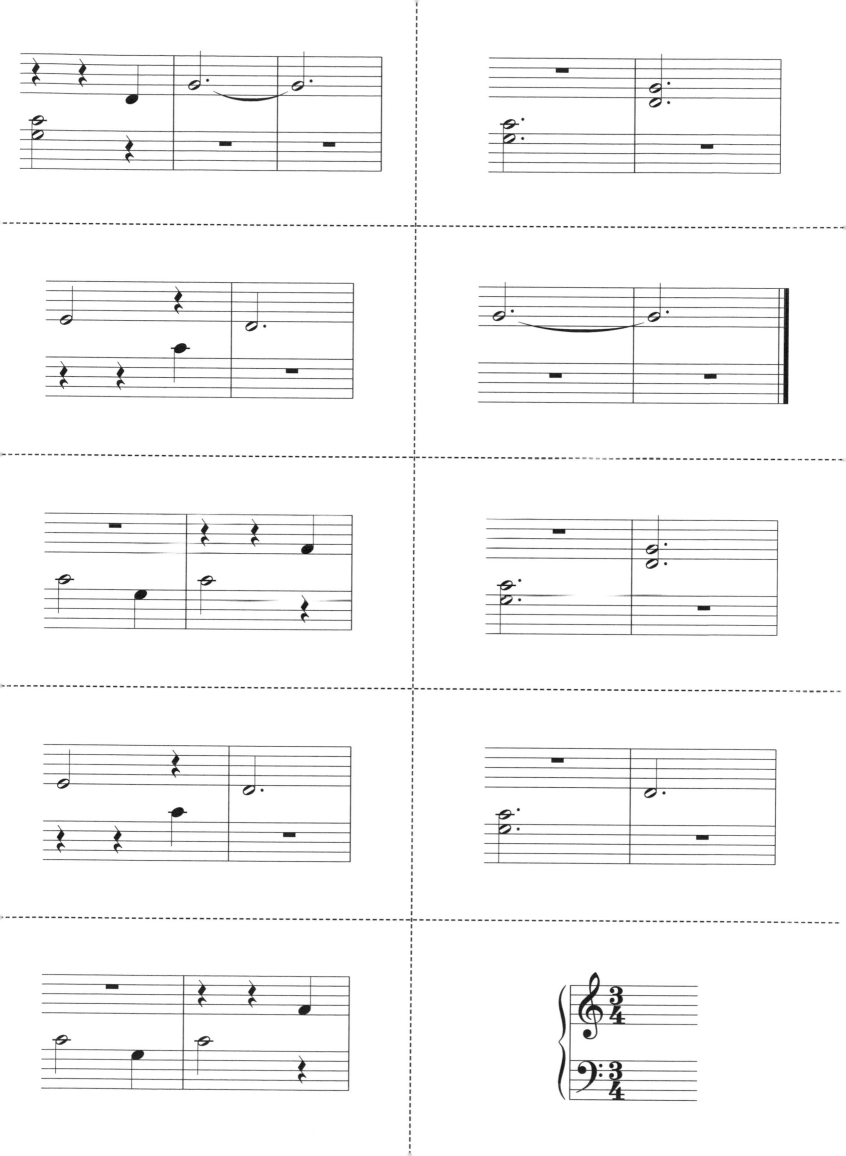

Bingo

(Lesson Book 2, pg. 14)

Finger Taps

As you listen to *Bingo*, tap the individual finger numbers. Tap either R.H., L.H. or hands together as indicated. Remember, *Bingo* begins with an UPBEAT.

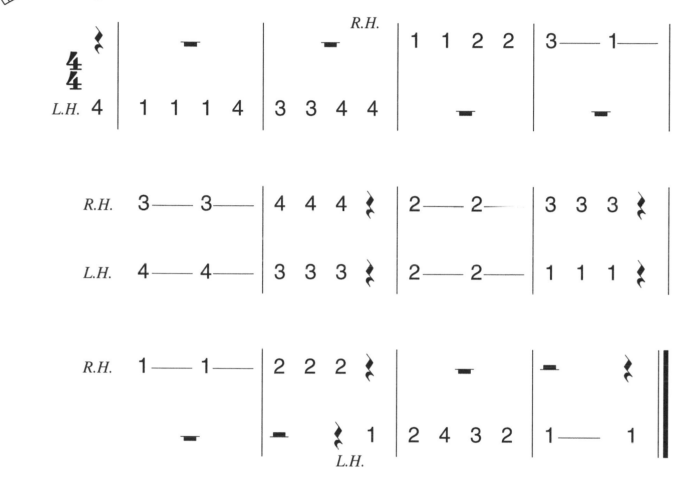

Reading Warm-up

Warm-ups help you learn the challenging parts of a piece. This warm-up uses only the first notes of each measure in measures 5-8.

1. Using your lesson book as a guide, write the finger numbers in the blank above or below each note.

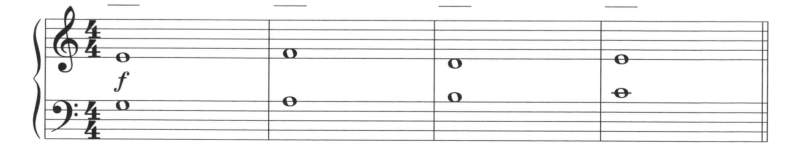

Travelling Along The Prairie

(Lesson Book 2, pg. 15)

Listen & Respond

As you listen to *Travelling Along The Prairie*, tap and count the following rhythm:

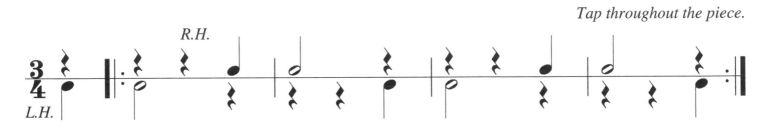

**Technique Tunes
by Katherine Glaser**

As you listen to the accompaniment to *Travelling Along The Prairie*, play the following **Technique Tune** one octave higher than written.

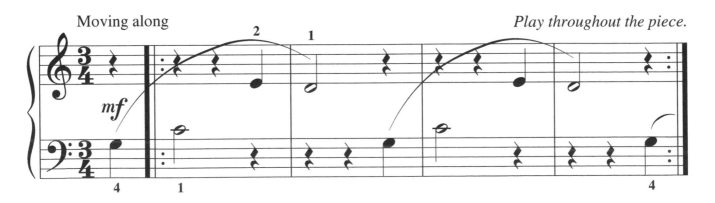

Imagine & Create

Get ready to improvise!

Place your hands in the *Travelling Along The Prairie* position and get ready to improvise a new piece titled *Orange Horizon*.

1. Practice playing this repeated accompaniment (ostinato) with your L.H.

2. After you can play the accompaniment easily, improvise a R.H. melody with the notes D E G A. Try playing your melody one octave higher.

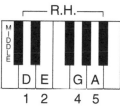

Orange Horizon

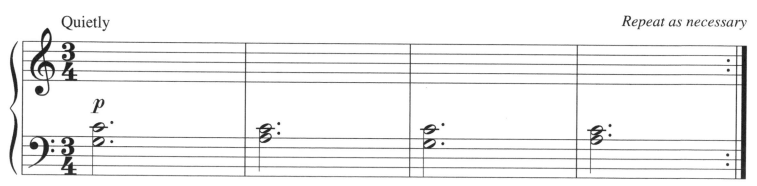

Hold damper pedal down throughout.

3. When you are ready to end your piece, rest your R.H. and let the L.H. accompaniment continue. Gradually fade away by playing softer and softer, slower and slower.

No One To Walk With

(Lesson Book 2, pg. 16)

  9

1. *No One To Walk With* has four phrases. Using your lesson book as a guide, add slurs ⌒ over each phrase below.

2. As you follow the score below, listen to the music and trace each phrase with your finger. Lift your wrist at the end of each phrase.

Phrase 1:

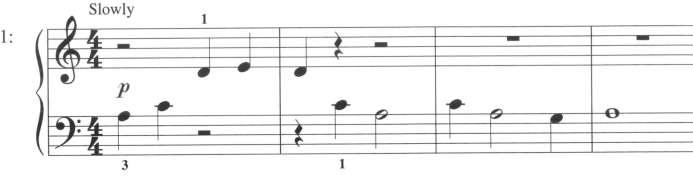

Phrase 2:

Phrase 3:

Phrase 4:

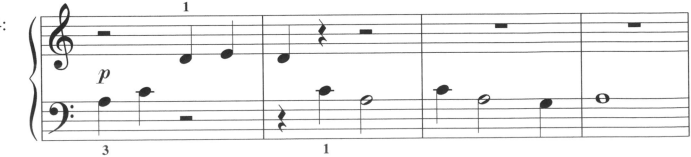

Expression Marks

Certain musical signs, such as 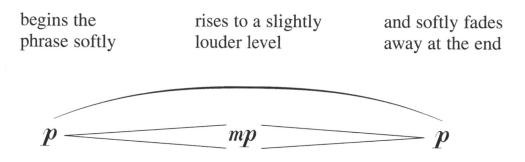 *(crescendo)* and *(decrescendo)*, tell us how to play the notes in a way that creates the mood of the music.

1. Sing *No One To Walk With* on "la" using one breath for each phrase. Be sure that your voice:

| begins the phrase softly | rises to a slightly louder level | and softly fades away at the end |

$$p \underset{}{\longrightarrow} \quad mp \quad \underset{}{\longrightarrow} \quad p$$

2. Imitate this effect on the piano by passing the sound from one finger to the next, creating a slight *crescendo* and *decrescendo* within each phrase.

Extra for Experts!

Study and compare the four phrases and circle the correct answers:

1. Which phrases are exactly alike?   1   2   3   4

2. Which phrase begins with an upbeat?   1   2   3   4

3. Which phrases include the melodic interval of a fourth?   1   2   3   4

Painted Rocking Horse

(Lesson Book 2, pg. 18)

 10

Many measures of the music look alike, but if you are a good detective, you will find the differences between them.

1. Play each of these examples:

Ex. 1

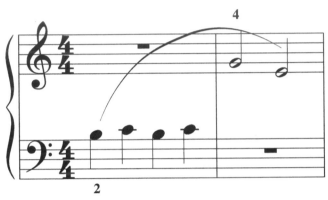

Ex. 2

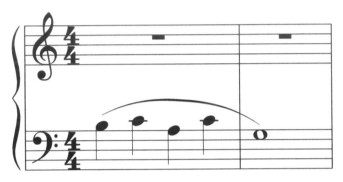

Ex. 3

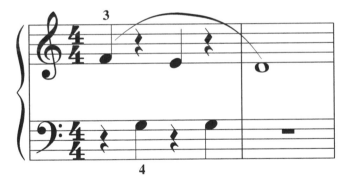

Ex. 4

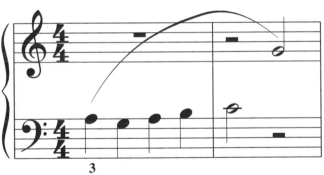

2. Circle the correct answers:

Which example begins in the R.H.?	1	2	3	4
Which example has no B in it?	1	2	3	4
Which example uses only the L.H.?	1	2	3	4
Which examples end on G?	1	2	3	4

18

Tick Tock The Jazz Clock

(Lesson Book 2, pg. 20)

Listen & Respond

As you listen to the accompaniment to *Tick Tock The Jazz Clock*, play Ex. 1 two octaves higher than written.

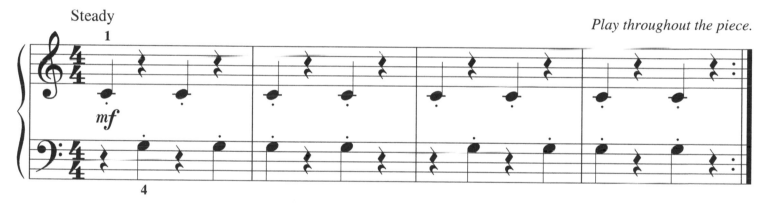

As you listen to the accompaniment again, play Ex. 2 two octaves higher than written.

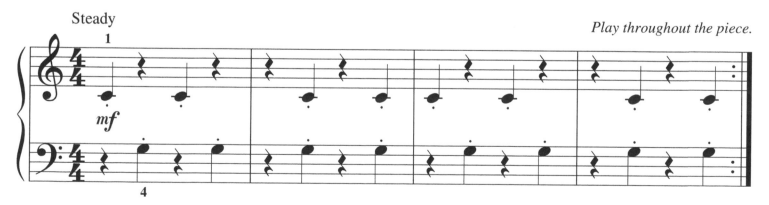

Read & Discover

1. Using your lesson book as a guide, compare the first measure of each line in *Tick Tock The Jazz Clock*.

   Which measures begin the same?   ☐ and ☐

   ☐ and ☐

Let's go on a Measure Hunt!

2. Tap and count each one-measure rhythm below.

   Each of these rhythms appears in the score of *Tick Tock The Jazz Clock*. How many times is each rhythm played? Write your answers in the boxes.

Imagine & Create

You can be the teacher!

Perhaps a family member or a friend would like to learn how to play the first line of *Tick Tock The Jazz Clock.*

1. To prepare for the lesson, circle the correct answers:

   Which hand plays G's only?   **right**   **left**

   Which hand plays C D E?   **right**   **left**

   Which finger of the right hand plays first?   **1**   **2**   **3**   **4**   **5**

   Which finger of the left hand plays first?   **1**   **2**   **3**   **4**   **5**

   What kind of touch should you use?   **legato**   **staccato**

2. Now you are ready to begin.
   Without looking at the score, show your student:

   WHERE to place his or her fingers on the keyboard.

   WHAT keys to play for this piece.

   WHEN to play each hand.

   HOW the piece sounds (staccato or legato).

Watercolors

(Lesson Book 2, pg. 22)

 🔊 **12**

Technique Tunes

As you listen to *Watercolors*, play the following **Technique Tune** three times:

1) as written
2) one octave higher
3) two octaves higher

Delicately

Hold down damper pedal throughout.

Note: As a duet, the teacher plays "Watercolors" two octaves higher, and the student plays the Technique Tune three times as written.

Imagine & Create

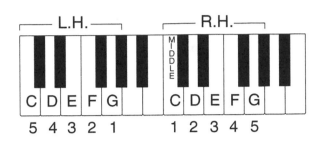

All that's missing is you!

Place your hands in the *Watercolors* hand position. As you listen to *Watercolors*, make up your own melody using the notes C D E F G in the empty measures. Play in the rhythm shown.

Circle Dance

(Lesson Book 2, pg. 23)

Technique Tunes

As you listen to *Circle Dance*, play the following **Technique Tune**. Connect the two-note slurs by using one continuous arm movement to pass the sound from one finger to the next. During each rest, relax your energy, keeping your fingers ready to play the next notes.

Note: As a duet, the teacher plays "Circle Dance" two octaves higher.

24

Reading Warm-up

Warm-ups help you learn the challenging parts of a piece. Once you can play this warm-up easily, you will be prepared to play *Circle Dance* from the score in your lesson book.

Basketball Bounce

(Lesson Book 2, pg. 24)

1. As you listen to *Basketball Bounce*, imitate the sound of a basketball bouncing back and forth between hands by tapping this rhythm:

Pass the Beat!

2. While one hand plays the beat, the other hand rests. Using your lesson book as a guide, write in the missing rests.

Read & Discover

Let's go on a Measure Hunt!

Using your lesson book as a guide, write the answers in the boxes below.

1. How many measures have an interval that moves **5** ↘ in the L.H.?

2. How many measures have an interval that moves ↗ **4** in the L.H.?

3. How many measures have the R.H. and L.H. playing the same notes an octave apart (in unison)?

Extra for Experts!

In the example below, the L.H. becomes a shadow of the R.H. and plays along in HARMONY.

Substitute this example for the last line of *Basketball Bounce!*

Great News!

(Lesson Book 2, pg. 26)

**Technique Tunes
by Katherine Glaser**

As you listen to *Great News!*, play this **Technique Tune** two octaves higher than written.

With excitement!

Play throughout the piece.

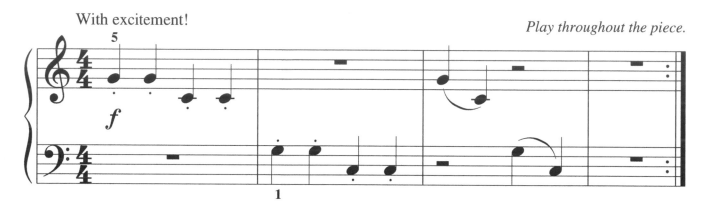

Read & Discover

1. Measure 13 uses the same notes as measure 14.
   Practice these measures until you can play them easily.

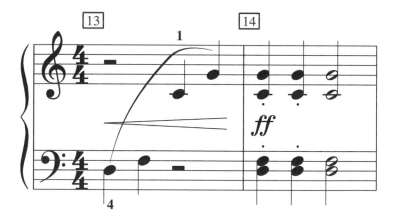

2. Circle the correct answers.

The intervals in measure 13 are:	**melodic**		**harmonic**	
The intervals in measure 14 are:	**melodic**		**harmonic**	
The L.H. plays an interval of a:	**2nd**	**3rd**	**4th**	**5th**
The R.H. plays an interval of a:	**2nd**	**3rd**	**4th**	**5th**

Brass Fanfare

(Lesson Book 2, pg. 27)

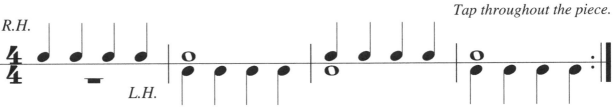

16 As you listen to *Brass Fanfare*, tap and count the following rhythm:

Tap throughout the piece.

Imagine & Create

Imagine you and three friends have formed a brass quartet made up of two trumpets and two trombones. Pictured below is a quartet score of the last line of *Brass Fanfare*.

1. Play each part separately to see what it sounds like.

2. Play the last line of *Brass Fanfare* from your lesson book with a *crescendo* from **ƒ** to **ƒƒ**, creating a triumphant ending!

Quiet Thoughts

(Lesson Book 2, pg. 29)

 17

Open your lesson book to the score of *Quiet Thoughts*. As you listen to the music:

1. Trace the phrases with your finger, remembering to lift your wrist at the end of each phrase.

2. Write the number of phrases in the box.

3. Which phrase echoes the one before it?

1. Play this version of *Quiet Thoughts* without the sharps (using the white keys only).

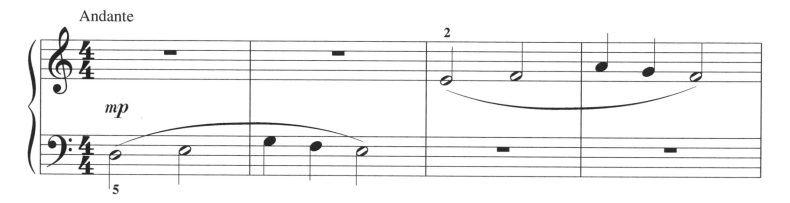

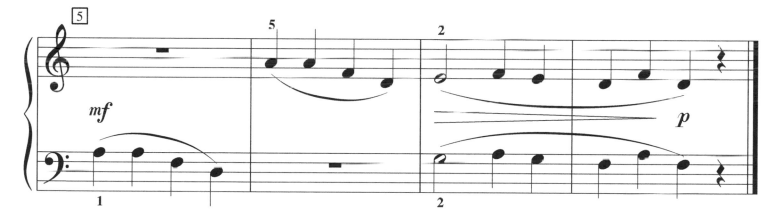

2. Practice writing a sharp in front of each note below.

Line-note sharps
(line cuts through the center of the ♯)

Space-note sharps
(center of ♯ fills the space)

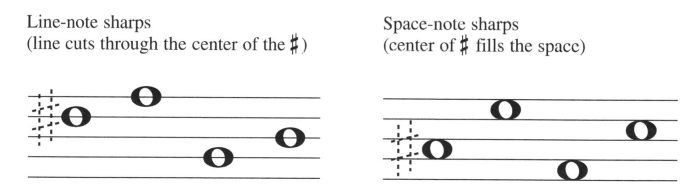

3. Add the missing sharps to the score of *Quiet Thoughts* above, using your lesson book as a guide.

4. To find out if you added all the sharps correctly, play your score of *Quiet Thoughts* to see if it sounds the same as the version in your lesson book.

A Little Latin

(Lesson Book 2, pg. 32)

1. *A Little Latin* loses some of its appeal when you play it without the B♭ in the L.H. Play this version of *A Little Latin* without the flats (using the white keys only).

Moderately fast

2. Practice writing a flat in front of each note below.

Line-note flats
(line cuts through the ♭)

Space-note flats
(♭ fills the space)

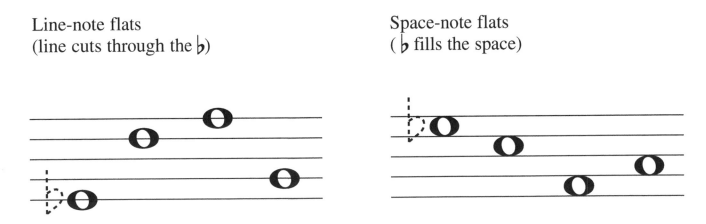

3. Add the missing flats to the score of *A Little Latin* above, using your lesson book as a guide.

4. To find out if you added all the flats correctly, play your score of *A Little Latin* to see if it sounds the same as the version in your lesson book.

Imagine & Create

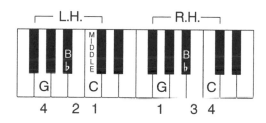 18

Let your hands talk to each other!

One way to create a piece is to trade phrases between your hands, playing first one hand and then the other. Make up your own piece using the following notes in both hands:

1. As you listen to the accompaniment to *A Little Latin*, play along as your R.H. asks a musical question and your L.H. answers back.

2. As your teacher plays the 12-bar blues accompaniment below, make up your own melody using the same notes in question and answer phrases between the hands.

Teacher Accompaniment

Moderately fast (♩ = 170)

Stompin'

(Lesson Book 2, pg. 33)

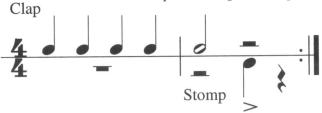

1. As you listen to *Stompin'*, clap the top part and stomp the bottom part with your left foot.

Repeat throughout the piece.

Clap

Stomp

Read & Discover

Eye spy!

Some of the notes in measures 10 and 12 are missing. Using your lesson book as a guide, fill in the missing notes.

Keep the beat!

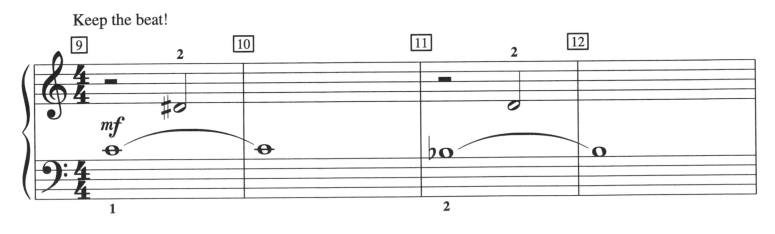

In measure 9,

(circle one)

the L.H. plays a **black / white** key,

the R.H. plays a **black / white** key.

In measure 11,

(circle one)

the L.H. plays a **black / white** key,

the R.H. plays a **black / white** key.

Imagine & Create

Get ready to improvise!

1. In jazz style, a repeated accompaniment pattern is called a **vamp**. Practice playing the L.H. vamp below.

Repeat as necessary

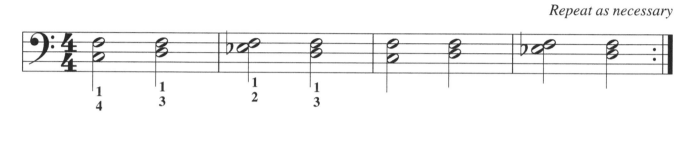

2. When you can play the L.H. vamp easily, use it as an introduction to your improvisation. Keep the vamp going as you improvise a melody in your R.H. using notes C D E♭ F.

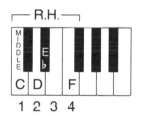

3. When you are ready to complete your improvisation, add the following ending:

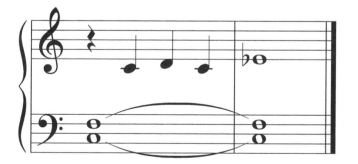

Inspector Hound

(Lesson Book 2, pg. 36)

20

Technique Tunes by Katherine Glaser

Make the two-note slurs sound "sneaky" by giving the first note of each slur more emphasis than the second. As you listen to *Inspector Hound*, play the two-note slurs in one arm movement.

Note: As a duet, the teacher plays "Inspector Hound" 8va higher and the student plays the Technique Tune 8va lower.

Read & Discover

Eye spy!

Using your lesson book as a guide, write the answers to the following questions in the boxes below.

1. How many different pitches does the R.H. play?

2. How many different pitches does the L.H. play?

Listen & Respond

Bayou Blues

(Lesson Book 2, pg. 37)

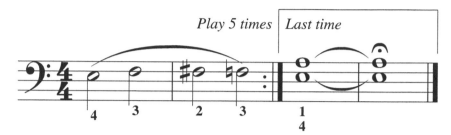

21

Imagine how it would feel to swing in a hammock on a hot summer day. As you listen to *Bayou Blues*, play this two-measure vamp in the LH:

Note: As a duet, the teacher plays "Bayou Blues" 8va higher.

Read & Discover

Match the lyrics!

Bayou Blues has four phrases in the R.H. Although each phrase uses the same three notes, each has a different rhythm.

1. Play each phrase in column A.

2. Draw lines matching the phrases in column A to the rhythm of the lyrics in column B.

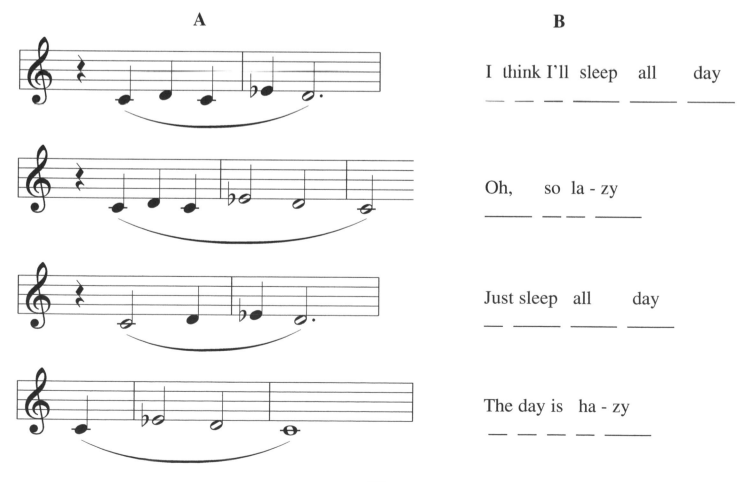

A	B
	I think I'll sleep all day
	Oh, so la - zy
	Just sleep all day
	The day is ha - zy

Imagine & Create

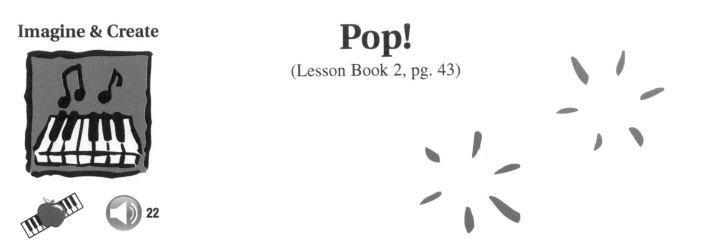

Pop!
(Lesson Book 2, pg. 43)

22

Create a new piece in A B A form!

1. As you listen to the accompaniment to *My Own Song on G A B C D*, play *Pop!* from your lesson book one octave higher than written. This is the A section of your piece.

A   Bouncy

mf   *Continue as written*

2. Using the notes G A B C D, make up your own B section by improvising for eight or more measures.

B

Improvise as you wish

3. Return to the beginning of *Pop!* (in jazz, that's called the "head") and play to the end of the piece.

A

mf   *Continue as written to end of song*

Listen & Respond

Jig

(Lesson Book 2, pg. 45)

 **23**

Technique Tunes

As you listen to *Jig*, play the following **Technique Tune**:

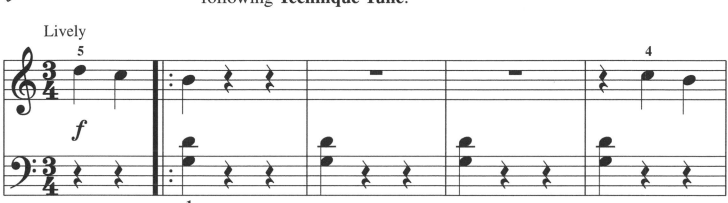

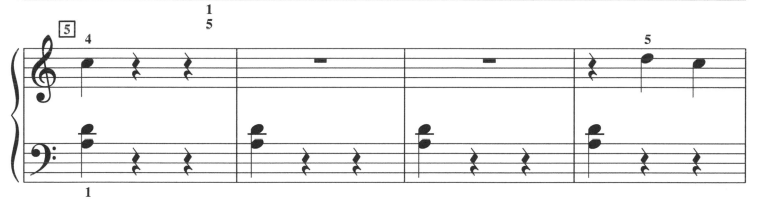

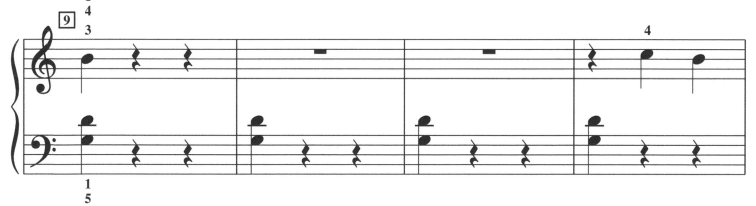

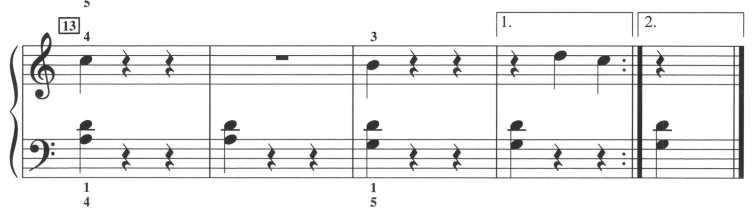

Note: As a duet, the teacher plays "Jig" 8va higher, and the student plays the Technique Tune 8va lower.

Go For The Gold

(Lesson Book 2, pg. 46)

Join the *Go For The Gold* orchestra!

1. As you listen to the accompaniment to *Go For The Gold*, imitate the sound of the piccolo parts. Play the following piccolo parts two octaves higher than written.

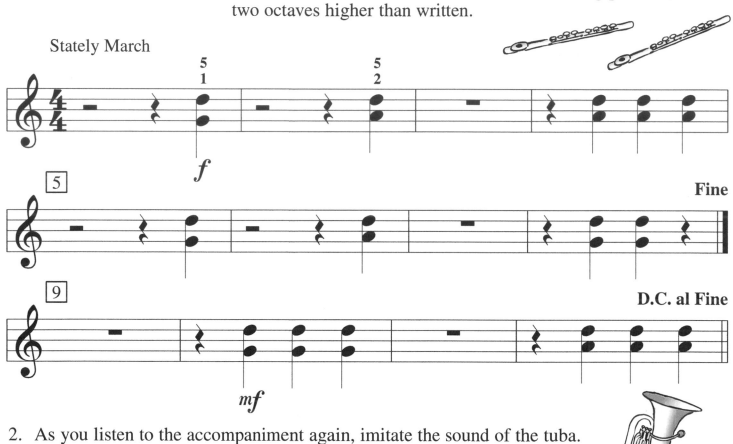

2. As you listen to the accompaniment again, imitate the sound of the tuba. Play the following tuba part two octaves lower than written.